The E-Commerce Cartel Presents:

eBay Profits Sales Business Model

Buying And Selling On eBay For Beginners

Written By
Delano B. Gurley

"It's Not A Matter Of IF It Works, Regardless of what it is, It will ALWAYS works if you work it."

-The E-Commerce Cartel

© Copyright 2014 by The Door 2 Success Publishing - All rights reserved. This document is geared towards providing exact and reliable information in regards to the topic and issue covered. The publication is sold with the idea that the publisher is not required to render accounting, officially permitted, or otherwise, qualified services. If advice is necessary, legal or professional, a practiced individual in the profession should be ordered.

From a Declaration of Principles, which was accepted and approved equally by a Committee of the American Bar Association and a Committee of Publishers and Associations.

In no way is it legal to reproduce, duplicate, or transmit any part of this document in either electronic means or in printed format. Recording of this publication is strictly prohibited and any storage of this document is not allowed unless with written permission from the publisher. All rights reserved.

The information provided herein is stated to be truthful and consistent, in that any liability, in terms of inattention or otherwise, by any usage or abuse of any policies, processes, or directions contained within is the solitary and utter responsibility of the recipient reader. Under no circumstances will any legal responsibility or blame be held against the publisher for any reparation, damages, or monetary loss due to the information herein, either directly or indirectly.

Respective authors own all copyrights not held by the publisher. The information herein is offered for informational purposes solely, and is universal as so. The presentation of the information is without contract or any type of guarantee assurance.

The trademarks that are used are without any consent, and the publication of the trademark is without permission or backing by the trademark owner. All trademarks and brands within this book are for clarifying purposes only and are the owned by the owners themselves, not affiliated with this document.

Enjoy The Wisdom In This Book:

For More:
@thedoor2success

All Wisdom Works If You Work It!

Table Of Contents

Assess The Market Demand For Your Product	12
Finding Out What's Selling	18
Finding The Right Product Price Point	19
Finding Money Making Deals At Garage Sales	21
Finding Money Making Deals Online	25
Top Wholesale Distributors	27
Optimizing Your Listing With Keywords	29
2 Keyword Ideas To Help Listings Stand Out	32
Presentation Is Everything	34
Provide The Customer With A Quality Experience	36
Steps To Great Customer Service	38
Stay Competitive In Your Target Market	42

Setting Up Your Payment Options	46
Some Important Keys to Know	51
The Process Of All Achievement	54
The Receipts: Proof This Works If You Work It	56

"Almost overnight, the internet has gone from a technical wonder, to a business must."

-Bill Schrader

The Definition of An eBay Sales Business Model

Under this direct sales business model, sales of products or services are made available to customers to generate revenue. **eBay Stores** allows you to set up an online storefront, that sells products at a set price or up for auction.

This business model is preferred by many **entrepreneurs** because through eBay they have access to an established audience of customers. An already waiting customer base, makes the hardest part of marketing ten times easier.

By listing your product with eBay, they take care of the shipping process, so all you have to do is pay the shipping, print off the label, package your "Sold Product" and send it off.

Businesses that have low start up fees and an already waiting customer base, makes making money a much faster and more enjoyable process. Just wait, you'll be addicted in no time.

STEP #1: Finding Your Product

Assess The Market Demand For Your Product

(Market Research)

Never attempt to sell a product that doesn't have demand and a solid customer base. By trying to sell a product with no demand you are setting yourself up to fail.

All it takes is a simple search around eBay's marketplace to find out exactly which products are in demand. A simple search of eBay's website will help you find exactly what category of products are getting the most attention.

Look At A Specific Products Number Of:

#1. Views

#2. Watchers

#3. Sales (# Sold)

As a seller you don't have to reinvent the wheel. By simply paying attention to what other's are successfully selling, you will place yourself in a great position to make money.

You can also use the "filters" to look at the "Buy It Now" filter to check the watchers for each item. High amounts of watchers means that a lot of people want that product.

Try to focus your energy on these popular products. If a specific niche works well for someone else, then you increase your probability of success with the same or similar product.

A. Find a product with a <u>High Profit Margin</u>

*Equation: Purchase Price - Resale Price = Profit

The profit margin is how much is left as Profit after you've subtracted expenses.

B. Find a <u>Popular Product</u>

The Key: Pay attention to categories with a lot of WATCHERS watching the products and a lot of SALES of the product you're prospecting.

Key Popular Categories Are:

- Fashion*
- Electronics*
- Collectibles
- Dolls and Bears
- Home and Garden
- Motors
- Pet Supplies*
- Sporting Goods
- Toys
- Antiques
- Computers/Tablets & Networking

TOP 3 Categories

C. Find a product that can be easily <u>Purchased and Repurchased</u> Repeatedly without interruption

*You must have a consistent source of supply of that product

*You must have consistency in that product

D. Find a product that <u>can be Repeatedly Re-listed</u> after the sale, because of past sales of the exact product

*This saves time and keeps the business repetitive and organized without thought

The Key: Also make sure this item does not violate eBay's limit on certain name brands like LV, Gucci, Burberry, Etc

E. Find a product that has a <u>Very Little Return Rate</u>

*This is accomplished through trial and error

TIP: Take very good pictures of the actual product along with stock photos. Do NOT only list with stock photos unless the product is exact to picture. Only use a stock photo as your first photo.

F. Make sure that the it is not obviously fake, a replica or violates eBay's selling policies. The item must be original or close to an original (inspired by) if selling replica merchandise.

Finding Out What's Selling

Do your Market Research

1. Look at the average price of your product being sold by other's

2. Is there any watchers on these products? Is there any demand for your product?

3. If there are a lot of people paying attention and "watching" a similar product you're selling, these are the prices you want to price towards.

*Look to price slightly below the competitions price, but be sure to have better pictures, description and presentation of your product.

Finding The Right Product Price Point

The best way to find the right price for a product is to look at the price your product is most commonly listed at. This makes it easy to find a good price that will compete with the prices of other's.

Pay attention to the items sold when you look at your competition. Their price point would be a great place to evaluate how much money you purchased the product for vs what the profit will be also.

If you're okay with taking small profits over a longer period of time, try competing price wise with your nearest competition. If you can, make the price just slightly less by a few cents or exactly the same.

Earning fast small profits over time vs slow lump sum profits for very short periods is going to be up to your personal preferences. But that'll be based solely on your goals, your personality and your drive.

Filters For Finding Price Comparisons:

1. Completed Auctions

*Completed auctions tell you what's sold

2. Completed and Sold

*Completed and sold tell you what price they've actually gone for

Finding Money Making Deals At Garage Sales

Step #1 Focus on figuring out what items you are looking for specifically

This means:

A. Do your research on items that have a high resale value

The Key: Be sure to focus on items that you have interest in, so you'll attune your attention to these items when you're out looking.

Fine Tuning Your Brain To Find Deals:

A quick lesson on the RAS: the reticular activation system is a part of the brain called the hypothalamus.

The hypothalamus is associated with filtering out information and awareness.

An Example of the RAS: When you buy a new car you start to see it everywhere, when before you bought the car you barely noticed them if at all. They were always there, it was just your brain is now paying attention to that car more because you told it to.

So by focusing your attention on specific products before you go out looking, you and your brain is ready to find whatever you're looking for. This is why doing your market research is so important. Because now your brain is focused on finding those specific items.

B. Make sure you know the resale value of what you're looking for, so you leave room for profit when you purchase the item

C. Check out nostalgia items that have ties to different generations. These items usually sell well and quickly

Step #2 Google Both Town Wide <u>Yard</u> Sale/Town Wide <u>Garage</u> sale

*This makes it more efficient if the sales are near each other

For example the one in MN is:

https://www.lifeinminnesota.com/minnesotas-city-wide-garage-sale-list/

*Find the one for your state

Step #3 Google the towns <u>Median Income</u>

*More affluent towns have more expensive and valuable items

Negotiations:

A. Silence is a huge negotiation tactic

*Ask for a lower price and be silent at their answer

Why: This starts people thinking if they want to get rid of it or not.

B. Ask for a lower price so there's room for negotiation

Why: By starting too high, you leave no room for a deal to be made in your favor

Finding Money Making Deals Online

The best way to be successful is to find wholesalers. The only issue if you're in the U.S. is that most of the wholesalers are located out of the country, such as China, India and other's.

So this means that you may get a great price for your product but it comes with risks and downside. Your products could get seized by customs, damaged during transport or given the wrong product.

The normal shipping is also a lot longer than US wholesalers and can take from 2 weeks to 1 month. But this is also based upon the shipping you pay, there is the option to pay for faster shipping if necessary.

Keep in mind that US sizes are different in other parts of the world. Be sure to check the Size Conversion Chart of that Country to determine sizes of your items to get the right item. There are multiple Manufacturers in the United States and also all over.

The list will start with the top 4 U.S Wholesale Distributors and then the top 3 Global Distributors. The specific wholesale marketplace you need will be determined by the product you are looking to sell.

Top Wholesale Distributors

Top US Distributors

1. https://www.bwanaz.com/ - Multi Categories

2. costco.com - Multi Categories

3. https://www.idwco.net/inventory - Alcohol

4. meetmable.com - Food

Top Overseas Distributors

1. alibaba.com - Multiple Categories

2. chinabrands.com - Multiple Categories

3. parisianwholesale.com - Clothing

4. wholesale7.com - Women's Clothing

5. paperdollwholesale.com - Women's Jewelry

STEP #2: Listing & Selling Your Product

Optimizing Your Listing With Keywords

It is very important as a Seller to remember that eBay is a search engine. If you notice after you list your product that it's not attracting any attention or views, watchers or sales, you may not be using the proper **KEYWORDS**.

A keyword is a specific search term that you use to rank your listing higher in a search engine. It helps to type in different words in eBay and see where the words take you.

Does the keyword you used go to the specific item that you are selling or looking to sell? If so you've found the right words to use in your listing, if not then continue to put words in eBay's search bar to find the proper words to use based upon other people's listings.

Another clue that your keywords are great, is when you list the item for sale the words you use should bring up other examples that you can use as a base for your listing.

With keywords also beware not to be in a highly competitive selling market. The keywords you use can be overly saturated with sellers already selling the same product, therefore creating keyword conflict.

This will lead to your listing being stuck at the bottom, especially in the beginning. When you have very few sales and customer reviews the goal has to be to get great reviews to increase your sales and customer credibility.

2 Keyword Ideas To Help Listings Stand Out

List your item as an Auction Style Listing - Right before your auction listing ends, eBay will put your listings near the top of the search results to make sure it gets the maximum amounts of market exposure.

eBay also does this to ensure that your item sells for the most amount of money possible, because eBay will benefit from the sale. So at the end of your auction you might see an influx of bids because of eBay's product placement algorithm.

If you find yourself struggling to get attention on your listing as a "Buy It Now" listing, try the strategy of resisting it as an Auction style Listing to increase the amount of eyes looking at your product.

Testing Your Product Titles - This step is a very useful step if you have a specific item in bulk and you are looking for a specific keyword that best fits your title. By testing 2 to 3 different titles, you will notice which one has the most views.

And now you can eliminate the ones that underperform. By listing a bulk product more than once with different search keywords, you will find the best one for your product.

Presentation Is Everything

A. <u>Take Great Pictures</u> of your product

The Key: Pictures of the products are what primarily make the sale. So make sure your pictures are cropped well and put them in a particular order.

#1. Use stock photo's as the main photo whenever possible

#2. Have pictures of the actual product

This prevents customer returns based on the photo and the product not matching. Because if the customer thinks they're getting a newer product based on the pictures, and a less quality item arrives they'll either leave you a bad review, or return the item, maybe both.

B. Once a sell is made be sure to <u>Ship The Item Quickly</u> with quality packaging to be sure the presentation of the item to the customer is on point

Tip: Quick shipping makes a difference in how the seller responds to the transaction

Provide The Customer With A Quality Experience

The level of a business' customer service can make the difference between a sale or a no sale. Always give your customer the best customer experience necessary to keep them as a prospective repeat customer.

Having great customer service along with a great product makes way for positive reviews. Positive reviews are the reference point for buyers. And they take the criticism of other's seriously when it comes to their purchase.

If a customer has a negative experience and leaves negative feedback for their purchase, your customer base will shrink. This is why you have to always make sure that the products you sell are high quality and ship quickly.

Not only will positive feedback lead to more sales, it leads to a high seller performance rating on eBay. A higher seller performance rating makes you more attractive as a seller for prospective buyers.

Steps To Great Customer Service

1. Always answer your buyer or perspective buyer in the same day or quickly most preferably

2. Have knowledge of the product that you are selling

3. Be respectful and empathetic to your customer

4. Go above and beyond what the customer asks

5. Use positive language even when attacked

Why: This gives you the ability to have eBay on your side in conflict. If you've insulted the person, when the eBay customer representative goes though the message records, your negativity will look bad on you as a seller.

6. The ability to read your customer

*Whenever you encounter a very negative buyer, this is a sign that they will be hard to satisfy and they are likely to return the product.

Remember to always provide the best possible customer service as possible. Gaining positive feedback reviews to your account is the easiest way to gain the trust of new and potential customers, as well increasing your seller performance as a whole on eBay.

A. The Customer is keeping you in business

The Key: Often in business we can forget that the customer has to be the center of your business

- Customer satisfaction is key to future buyers

- Customer Reviews based upon bad customer service or a misleading product will result in less sales to no sales

- Customers pay attention to your reviews

- Great reviews increase sales, while bad reviews decrease sales

B. Always answer your buyers questions back in a timely manner.

The Key: Courteous and pleasant transactions keep buyers coming back for more. Because we all want to feel good about our purchase, and feel like the seller cares about our satisfaction.

Stay Competitive In Your Target Market

Know who your competition is for your product and what either sets their product apart or what sets your product apart from theirs, based on who's the best selling merchant.

You must know what separates you from the competition to compete in the marketplace. If they are selling more product than you, what is their competitive edge?

Is it their presentation? The photo's, their description or are their keywords better than yours? Do they have more watchers than you for the same product? If so it is your job to stay competitive to always upgrade your business.

If you are the major seller, how are you going to stay in that lane, especially when competitors challenge your product with better prices? How do you improve your presentation, price and even the product?

These very important factors will have a direct impact on your sales, your competitiveness, your profits and what makes your product more attractive to the prospective buyer.

These Factors Are:

<u>Factor #1</u>. How does your price match up? Is it cheaper, better quality for the price, faster or free shipping?

<u>Factor #2</u>. How does your description hold up? Is it detailed and precise? Is their keywords being used to attract the customer?

<u>Factor #3</u>. Do you have the best and cheapest price?

<u>Factor #4</u>. Is the quality of your product better?

<u>Factor #5</u>. Do you have a quicker delivery time? Or is your shipping free?

STEP #3: Getting Payment

Setting Up Your Payment Options

A. Set up Payments directly through eBay

1. Go to your eBay account settings

2. Go down to the SELLING Category and choose Seller Account

3. Follow the directions to set up your payment account directly on eBay

4. This method will ask you to use your bank account to manage transactions

The Setup:

A. Set up one specifically for your eBay Business

#1. Use your personal bank account

Or

#2. Set up a business account for eBay payments

STEP #4: Buy Only From Credible Sellers

A. Buy products from Credible Sources ONLY

Why: You make the odds greater that you'll be unsatisfied with the purchase

Credible sources criteria include:

#1. A great seller rating

#2. Plenty of successful sales

#3. Great reviews from past buyers

#4. Quality products

#5. Timely Communication

B. They MUST be reliable

Once you find the right seller for the merchandise you're seeking, these things must be consistent:

#1. Shipping time

#2. Merchandise quality

#3. Reliable Communication

#4. Return Policies and refund time

Some Important Keys to Know

1. Do not take the money out of the bank until the buyer has received the item and is satisfied with their order

*This puts you in a position to have to pay the money back and maybe lose your selling and PayPal privileges

2. If you sell replica products you take a risk of being banned and negative feedback

*If your product violates eBays selling policy, you will be subject to a 30 day or more selling suspension

3. Do not sell products that puts other's health or safety at risk

*You have to sell with a moral compass. Don't sell products that you would not use yourself

4. Respond to people's messages in a timely manner

*When someone spends their money with you, they are trusting that they will be able to interact with you respectfully and timely

5. Be clear in your own motives

*Selling something of low quality to get money will end up in a refund. So why waste your time, make the exchange mutually beneficial

6. Returns are part of the game

Key: When a buyer wants to return an item, ask them to make sure it is the original condition. If not you do not have to take the return. Contact eBay after this conversation and see the message that it was worn or used

*Return a buyers money back as soon as you receive the product back in the original condition

7. Save and Reinvest some of your profits

*Reinvest a certain amount of money based upon profits back into the purchase of more products and materials

8. Keep a ledger of your purchases and the profits

*A small notebook is all you need to keep track of what the item cost, sold for, sale fees and final profit of each product

*This helps you keep track on a daily, weekly, monthly and yearly basis of your profits

The Process Of All Achievement

1. **Learn The Process**

*Do the research and put in the hours necessary to feel confident in your knowledge of the area you seek success

2. **Love The process**

*You must fall in love with the process. If you don't love something you won't stay loyal to it.

3. **Trust The process**

*Once you find the way, have faith that this process will reap the results that you desire. The level of your faith will determine your level of achievement

4. Repeat the Process

*A successful process repeated over and over, brings a consistent outcome of success. Once you have the formula, rinse and repeat.

5. Share The Process

*Once you find the way, share the process with those who want to learn. Be sure to only share the process with those who are willing to invest in the process themselves.

The Receipts: Proof This Works If You Work It

"It's Not A Matter Of IF It Works, Regardless of what it is, It will ALWAYS works if you work it."

- The E-Commerce Cartel

We know this works and we know you need receipts understandably I do too. This is just one year as a side hustle. Only time spent was creating the listing, taking pictures of my product and then, checking similar prices to know my price points, then listing the item.

Once you get the process down it takes 20 minutes and you have the rest of the day to work your other job. If you go full time you could easily double this $16,000. 00 into 30,000.00 or much much more.

Receipts

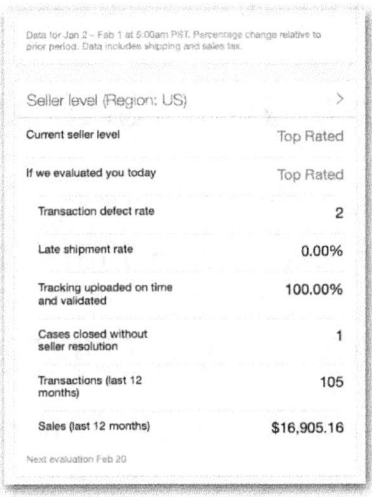

Avg Monthly Total: $1,654.37

Yearly Total: $16,905.16

If You Received Useful Tools In This Information, Please Give Me A

4-5 Star Rating!

This serves as a reward for an author. It takes hours and months, sometimes years of no pay to put together books for the purpose of sharing information you see as important to the world.

Please just take out a minute of your time and please leave a quick positive review. If you didn't receive any value from this book then dm me on instagram @thedoor2success to tell me why.

Either way, Thank you tremendously for taking out the time to read this information and knowledge. If you really took this information seriously and you applied the key principles into your daily life, I KNOW you are seeing results.

So again, I thank you for your interest in learning and any investment in applied knowledge will always be a winning investment.

THANK YOU FOR READING

NOTES

www.ingramcontent.com/pod-product-compliance
Lightning Source LLC
Chambersburg PA
CBHW070827220526
45466CB00002B/771